VANCOUVER

photo album

ALTITUDE
PUBLISHING
Canadian Rockies/Vancouver

Copyright © 1997 Altitude Publishing Canada Ltd.
1500 Railway Avenue, Canmore, Alberta Canada T1W 1P6

Canadian Cataloguing in Publication Data
Grobler, Sabrina, 1972-
Vancouver photo album
ISBN 1-55153-129-1
1. Vancouver (B.C.)--Pictorial works. I. Title.
FC3847.37.G762 1997   971.1'33'00222   C97-910021-6
F1089.5.V22G762 1997

Printed in Canada 🍁
by Friesen Printers, Altona Manitoba

Production
Art Direction and Design ....Stephen Hutchings
Project Management ....Sharon Komori
Production Management ....Mark Higenbottam
Financial Management ....Laurie Smith
Sales Management ....Scott Davidson

Altitude GreenTree Program
Altitude Publishing will plant in Canada twice as many trees as were used in the manufacturing of this product.

Front Cover: An aerial view of Coal Harbour, Stanley Park and the North Shore
Back Cover: Vancouver skyline and English Bay

PHOTOGRAPHY
Image Network Inc. is pleased to be associated with Altitude Publishing Canada Ltd. in the production of *Vancouver Photo Album*. All images in this book are courtesy of Image Network Inc., and are available by contacting Image Network Inc. at:

Image Network Inc.,
16 East 3rd Avenue, Vancouver, British Columbia, V5T 1C3
tel: (604) 879-2533 • fax: (604) 879-1290 • e-mail: twood@direct.ca

Image Network Inc. photographers include:
Owen Broad (6-7, 9, 10, 14, 26, 29b, 37a, 40-41, 51b, 54a/b, 56b),
Gary Fiegehen (18b), **Al Harvey** (front cover, 2-3, 8, 11, 13, 17b, 21, 32b, 33, 35, 42, 45, 47b, 55a/b, 58, 59b, 61a), **Cameron Heryet** (16, 22-23, 36a), **Images BC** (12, 25b, 37b, 59a, 61b, 62), **Kharen Hill** (19, 24, 38, 39, 48, 49b, 60), **Robert Karpa** (15a),
Peter Langer (18a, 53), **Tim Matheson** (17a, 43, 46, 63, back cover),
Stuart McCall (20a, 27, 47a, 49a), **Ron Sangha** (20b, 25a), **Brian Sprout** (5, 15b, 28, 29a, 32a, 34, 36b, 50, 52, 56a, 57), **Eero Sorila** (30-31), **Bill Tice** (51a).

Vancouver skyline

Contents

VANCOUVER

The "Crown Dynasty" leaving Vancouver

Captain George Vancouver, who was part of Captain James Cook's expedition to Vancouver Island's west coast in 1778, arrived again in 1792 in search of the Northwest Passage. Fifty-one years later, Fort Victoria was founded by the Hudson's Bay Company and by British colonial officials on the island's coast. Over the course of the next few decades, it became a sawmill town with a burgeoning economy. In 1867, John Deighton or "Gassy Jack", as locals called the colorful story-teller, built a saloon on the waterfront to service the laborers who worked in the logging camps. Deighton is the namesake of Gastown, the original business core which was christened "Granville" in 1870.

The beginning of Granville's journey to becoming the metropolis we know as Vancouver was its designation as the western terminus of the

Bill Reid's *The Jade Canoe* is the centrepiece of the Vancouver airport

CPR in 1886. It was William Cornelius Van Horne, the General Manager of the CPR, who named Granville *Vancouver*. The railway brought British immigrants from the east who saw an opportunity to profit from the city's rapid commercial expansion. Vancouver's economy experienced another boom in 1898, when the Klondike gold rush attracted still more settlers. Echoes of Vancouver's atmosphere at the turn of the century are still apparent in the Edwardian era suburbs with their lovely picket-fenced houses, and in the cobblestone streets of Gastown, where the original buildings still stand. Similarly, Vancouver's indigenous populations—the Coast Salish, Nootka and Kwakiutl people are honored by local artisans and historic sites which illustrate their cultural heritage.

By the time of the first world war, Vancouver's international profile as a land of bounty and natural splendor had been established. Vancouver's population of 100,000 enjoyed an opera house, theatres, a streetcar system and the sight of luxury ocean liners in its ports. Today, the city's population has swelled to 1.8 million. Its 45 museums and historical sites, fes-

Cruise ship at Canada Place

tivals, Stanley Park attractions and botanical gardens are among the diversions Vancouver has to offer. Skiers, climbers, kayakers and cyclists enjoy mild temperatures year round, and can enjoy their activities within the city limits.

Vancouver's skyline is as diverse and exciting as its natural environment. The sandstone and granite buildings, built during the prosperous turn of the century, exude the self-assurance of a city that was growing aware of its potential.

The neoclassical style of the Vancouver Art Gallery, is a fine example. The later art deco style of the Marine building contrasts beautifully with the traditional austerity of this former courthouse. The adjacent Robson Square, with its magnificent law courts, typifies the architectural elegance of Vancouver's contemporary buildings. The translucent sails of Canada Place (the Canadian pavilion during Expo '86), the Pan-Pacific Hotel and the Science Centre—reflecting the future in its design and the North

The magnificent sails at Canada Place

Canada Place at night

Shore mountains in its glittering surface—are noteworthy examples. The design of City Hall reflects the same multiplicity of forms which characterizes Vancouver's downtown core. While the art deco detail in its façade speaks to the 20th Century, its columns and freizes gesture toward the neoclassical fashion of its past, indicating that Vancouver is a city in which history reverberates.

Vancouver captures the imagination of the visitor like no other city can. Its images revisit the traveller long after s/he has left it. Its character has many faces. Vancouver is at once the pulsating, entrepreneurial business core that made Expo '86 a success, the urban site closest to the last of Canada's virgin rainforests, a tapestry of languages and ethnic practices, a gateway to international trade and a viewpoint from which seals can be seen playing in the nearby harbour. Vancouver imposes no limits, and has thus become a favorite destination of artists, athletes and travellers alike.

An aerial view of Canada Place

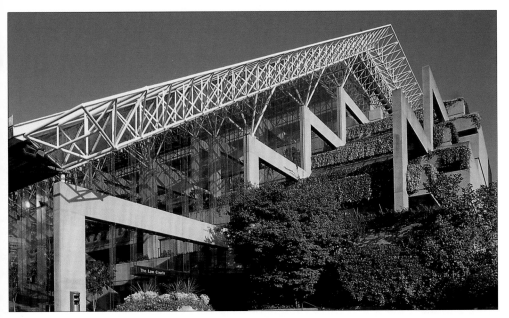

Vancouver Courthouse

Robson Square

Vancouver Art Gallery and Hotel Vancouver

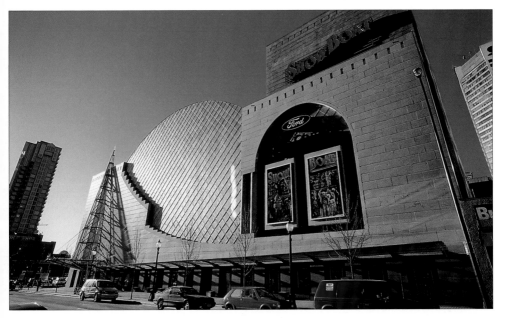

Ford Theatre

Fireworks at English Bay

Vancouver Public Library

Gateway at the Chinese Cultural Centre

Dragon Dance to celebrate Chinese New Year

Dr. Sun Yat-Sen Classical Chinese Garden

B.C. Place Stadium and GM Place

NBA game at GM Place

ATTRACTIONS

Robson Street at night

Over three million tourists are attracted to this mountain seascape per year, despite its reputation for being rainy. In fact, Vancouver receives less rain than does the east coast, and its mild winters are due to its location in warm Pacific airstreams. The city's mild climate and consequent lush vegetation are largely responsible for its widespread appeal.

Pacific Spirit Park is part of the University Endowment Lands, 1000 ha (2500 acres) of forest which dates back five hundred years. Here, it is easy to forget that you are in one of the nation's largest cities. Its lovely trails provide perfect terrain for horseback riding, mountain biking and jogging. Vancouver's green refuges are the

overleaf: **Vancouver skyline at sunset**

Vancouver City Hall

Vancouver City Hall at night

City skyline from Port of Vancouver

Gastown street scene

domain of the western red cedar, spruce, hemlock and the giant Douglas fir, which can grow to a height of 60 metres (200 feet).

While much of the city's architecture reflects its modernity and innovative flavour, Vancouver's history is manifest in every countour of the cityscape. The nostalgic atmosphere of Gastown, for example, reminds visitors of the richness of Vancouver's past. The ancient Douglas fir, the totem poles scattered throughout the city, the turn-of-the-century storefronts of Gastown, the futuristic Science Centre—all represent the historical layers which have contributed to Vancouver's unique heritage.

Gastown steam clock

Vancouver Museum and Planetarium

Plaza of Nations Buildings

Vancouver Museum and Planetarium at night
overleaf: **Science Centre**

Seawall at English Bay

Springtime at English Bay

ENGLISH BAY

English Bay Beach

Since the West End was developed in the 1890s, English Bay has been one of Vancouver's most popular attractions. English Bay and the beaches which border Stanley Park are a nexus of recreation and commerce. While visitors and locals come here to enjoy sunbathing, windsurfing, picnics and evening strolls before sunset, English Bay also affords a view of the barges. Great freighters laden with grain, fish and other goods make their way across the bay to the Port of Vancouver. In summer and winter alike, Vancouver's beaches are festive gathering places. Each summer, the Benson & Hedges Festival of Fire attracts thousands to the sandy shores to watch the fireworks. The Folk Festival on Jericho Beach features salmon barbecues, music and dancing. At Christmas, carolers on yachts and sailboats serenade the beaches of False Creek and English Bay, and some 2,000 people jump into English Bay to participate in the annual "Polar Bear" swim on New Year's Day.

GRANVILLE ISLAND

Granville Island

False Creek, in which Granville Island is located, was once the industrial heart of Vancouver. Between 1914 and 1916, nearly one million cubic metres of mud was transferred from the creek to increase the area of the sand bar. In 1979, the warehouses which for fifty years produced only heavy machinery were converted to house the Granville Island Public Market.

Today, this former industrial centre is a hotbed of arts and leisure. The market offers an astonishing variety of fresh local produce, seafood and the wares of local craftspeople. Granville Island boasts over thirty studios and galleries in which textiles, jewellry, pottery, paintings and sculptures are produced. The Kids Only Market is a veritable haven of puppet studios, interactive arts, toy workshops and bookstores. On the waterfront is the Arts Club Theatre Complex, where colorful dance, musical and dramatic productions are staged.

Granville Island at night

Marina at Granville Island

Vancouver's west end from Granville Island

Burrard Street Bridge

Aquabus in False Creek

TROUT, SALMON AND CHAR OF NORTH AMERICA

Flower shop in Granville Island Public Market

Seafood stand in Granville Island Public Market
overleaf: **City skyline from Vanier Park**

ISLAND PARK WALK

STANLEY PARK

Totem poles at Brockton Point in Stanley Park

Stanley Park is a land mass of over 40 hectares (1000 acres) which juts into Burrard Inlet.Named after Lord Stanley, the Governor General at the time of the park's formation in 1889, it was designated for "the use and enjoyment of peoples of all colours, creeds and customs, for all time." This wilderness area, located in the heart of the city, offers the visitor a wide range of recreational amenities. It is bordered by the Seawall, a paved, 10.5-kilometre pathway from which both pedestrians and cyclists enjoy a lovely view of the seacape. This trail connects the recreational areas: an aquarium, rowing and yacht clubs, playing fields, picnic areas, playgrounds, beaches, an open-air theatre, monuments and totem poles. On the shores of Stanley Park are Sunset Beach, English Bay, the busy Second Beach and Third Beach.

Stanley Park seawall

Running through the park are miles of forest trails which are frequented by cyclists and joggers.

Among Stanley Park's main attractions are Lost Lagoon, a haven for bird watchers with its freshwater sanctuary for waterfowl, the Vancouver Aquarium in Stanley Park, which houses marine life from Arctic Canada to the Amazon Rainforest, and a miniature railway which features a replica of the first CPR locomotive to journey to Vancouver in 1887. Along the Seawall and east of the Harding Memorial are two "vertical condominiums" for the great blue herons which frequent the area in spring and early summer.

One of the principal villages of the Coast Salish people in the late 1700s, whose villages on the shores of Burrard Inlet date over five thousand years, was located in what is now Stanley Park. The Brockton Point Totems are an impressive collection of totem poles which feature the whale, wolf, eagle and bear which were an integral part of First Nations people's everyday lives. Crafted from western red cedar, the totem poles of the Salish, Haida and Kwakiutl can be found near the Lions Gate Bridge, in front of the Maritime Museum, and above all, in the magnificent Museum of Anthropology.

The interior of the park is densely forested and contains a network of bike and foot paths. In the centre of it is Beaver Lake, a picturesque natural-state pond surrounded by cattails.

Stanley Park is a protected area which provides locals with a quick escape from the humdrum of the workplace. For visitors, a day in the park is a welcome pause in the whirl of activity that characterizes the visit of the enthusiastic sightseer.

Walking bridge at Stanley Park near Second Beach

Cherry Blossoms in Stanley Park

Horse & Carriage Tour through Stanley Park

Vancouver Rowing Club at Coal Harbour

Lost Lagoon at night

Beluga whale at the Vancouver Aquarium

English Bay at sunset

Stanley Park seawall in the fall

Lions Gate Bridge

Stanley Park Seawall

GARDENS & BEACHES

Queen Elizabeth Park

Vancouver is replete with magnificent gardens which represent a number of the city's ethnic groups. Among the gardens at the University of British Columbia are the Asian, Alpine, Winter, Contemporary and Physick gardens, the latter of which represents a typical sixteenth century English medicinal herb garden. The Nitobe Memorial Garden, with its carp-stocked lake, tea garden, waterfalls and bridges reflects the Japanese philosophical principles of Zen and Shintoism. Vancouver also boasts the only authentic classical garden ever constructed outside China. The Dr. Sun Yat-Sen Classical Chinese Garden's imported rock formations and hand-fired Chinese roof tiles reflect the botanical fashion which prevailed during the Ming Dynasty.

VanDusen Botanical Gardens

Jericho Beach

In 1951, Princess Elizabeth planted the first tree of what was to become the Bloedel Conservatory in Queen Elizabeth Park. Situated at the highest point in the city atop the "little mountain," it features a plexiglass dome which covers a small desert and a jungle complete with tropical birds.

Vancouver's largest garden is the VanDusen Botanical Garden, the pride of which are its hedge maze and 942 varieties of rhododendron. Also a popular destination is Stanley Park's Rose Gardens. Many visitors who discover it unexpectedly delight in the scent of its 275 varieties of roses.

Beach Avenue

Wreck Beach

Saltwater Kitsilano Pool

A stroll along Kitsilano Beach

Kitsilano neighbourhood

NORTH SHORE

Capilano Suspension Bridge

Lovers of the outdoors gravitate year round to Vancouver's North Shore. In the winter months, the chairlift carries alpine skiers up Grouse Mountain to the chalet above. The ski hill can be seen from the city, particularly when night skiers enjoy the illuminated slopes. During the eight minute Skyride by gondola which terminates 3700 feet (1128 metres) above the city, a lovely view of the city unfolds.

At the mountain's base is Capilano River Regional Park. Hikers enjoy a stroll around Blue Grouse Lake or up to Goat Mountain in the

Capilano Suspension Bridge

Lonsdale Quay

Vancouver skyline at night from the North Shore

summer. Nearby, the thrilling venture across the Capilano Suspension Bridge provides a breathtaking view of the river, 230 feet (69 metres) below. While crossing the canyon, visitors can see the waterfalls below and the ancient Douglas firs which tower above the forest on the other side of the bridge. The trails in the Capilano area are well marked, and interpretive signs are posted intermittently along the way, making for an interesting and informative excursion.

Grouse Mountain, aerial view

Grouse Mountain Skyride

FESTIVITIES

One of many bridges connecting Vancouver and the Lower Mainland

Vancouver, it seems, is always in the midst of a celebration. In summer and autumn alone, the city's festivals attract thousands of visitors to the downtown core. In May, Vanier Park is the site of the Vancouver Children's Festival, the largest children's performing arts festival in North America. In June, hundreds of international jazz and blues bands perform at over twenty venues for the du Maurier Jazz Festival. Also in June is the magnificent Chinese Dragon Boat Festival, an international race which takes place in False Creek. The Vancouver Folk Music Festival occupies six stages in Jericho Park in mid July, and at the end of the same month, English Bay is illuminated by the spectacular fireworks display of the Benson & Hedges Symphony of Fire. In Vancouver's Japantown, the Powell Street Festival features

Japanese food, music and dancing. Authentic tea ceremonies are also performed during this event.

Vancouver hosts a number of events for sports lovers, such as regattas, marathons and bike races. Each Labour Day weekend, the Vancouver Indy attracts thousands of enthusiastic spectators to the track around the former Expo site.

In autumn, the city's "alternative" scene reaches its peak. In late September and early October, the Vancouver Fringe, International Film and International Writers' Festivals draw the city's attention to the arts which, during the rest of the year, tend to have a relatively low profile.

With the advent of each festival emerges a different side of Vancouver's character. The festivals provide locals and visitors with an opportunity to celebrate their own interests and ethnic backgrounds, as well as to explore other cultures and hobbies. Vancouver's gatherings, like its social climate and its natural setting, stimulate personal growth in inhabitants and visitors that is both enriching and memorable.